TAMPA BAY
RAYS

by Paul Bowker

Published by ABDO Publishing Company, 8000 West 78th Street, Edina, Minnesota 55439. Copyright © 2011 by Abdo Consulting Group, Inc. International copyrights reserved in all countries. No part of this book may be reproduced in any form without written permission from the publisher. SportsZone™ is a trademark and logo of ABDO Publishing Company.

Printed in the United States of America,
North Mankato, Minnesota
112010
012011

 THIS BOOK CONTAINS AT LEAST 10% RECYCLED MATERIALS.

Editor: Chrös McDougall
Copy Editor: Nicholas Cafarelli
Interior Design and Production: Craig Hinton
Cover Design: Craig Hinton

Photo Credits: Rob Carr/AP Images, cover; Chris O'Meara/AP Images, 1, 39, 47; Wilfredo Lee/AP Images, 4, 43 (middle); Julie Jacobson/AP Images, 7; Mike Carlson/AP Images, 8, 11; Scott Audette/AP Images, 12, 42 (top); Robert Azmitia/AP Images, 15; Steve Nesius/AP Images, 16, 19, 30, 35, 36, 40, 43 (top and bottom); Jim Rogash/AP Images, 20; Eric Gay/AP Images, 23, 42 (middle); John Dunn/AP Images, 24; Elise Amendola/AP Images, 26, 32, 42 (bottom); Katsumi Kasahara/AP Images, 29; Kathy Willens/AP Images, 44

Library of Congress Cataloging-in-Publication Data
Bowker, Paul, 1954-
  Tampa Bay Rays / by Paul Bowker.
      p. cm. — (Inside MLB)
  Includes index. 9-3-14
  ISBN 978-1-61714-060-0
  1. Tampa Bay Rays (Baseball team)—History—Juvenile literature. I. Title.
  GV875.T26B69 2011
  796.357'640975965—dc22
                                      2010045213

TABLE OF CONTENTS

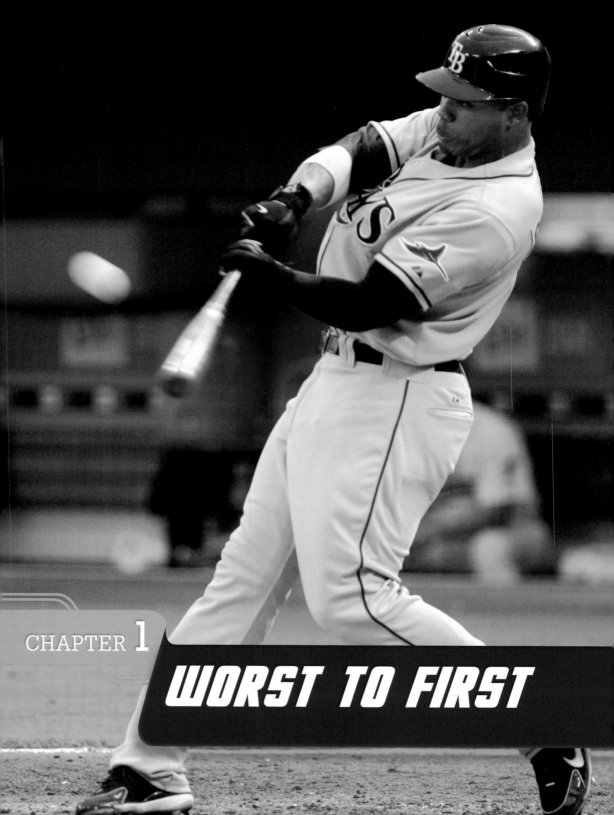

CHAPTER 1

WORST TO FIRST

The Tampa Bay Devil Rays hardly had a storied history going into the 2008 season. The team had joined the American League (AL) in 1998. Yet the Rays had finished last in the powerful AL East Division in all but one season. After 10 years of baseball, they had yet to finish a season with a winning record.

The team had tried to attract fans over the years by signing big stars such as Wade Boggs and Jose Canseco. However, both players were near the end of their careers by the time they arrived in Tampa. The team hired Joe Maddon as manager in 2006. But they still lost 197 games over the next two seasons.

As a result, attendance had plummeted at the team's home ballpark, Tropicana Field. The team attracted only 1.3 million fans in 2007. That was less than 14,000 per game. No team in the AL had fewer fans that

Carl Crawford's potent bat helped the Rays make their first playoff appearance in 2008.

season. The fans who did show up did not see many wins. The team finished the season 66–96.

The team decided to make some changes after the 2007 season. For one, it changed its name from the Devil Rays to the Rays. It also changed the primary color of its uniforms from green to blue. More than 7,000 fans cheered when the changes were announced at a rally in downtown Tampa.

What's in a Name?

After 10 losing seasons, Devil Rays owner Stuart Sternberg wanted a name change and new team colors. No more Devil Rays. More than 1,000 suggestions rolled in. Sternberg and other club officials eventually settled on dropping the "Devil" from the name since the team was known around town as the Rays anyway. The new team name and a logo featuring a bright yellow sunburst and a dominant blue color debuted in 2008. A few of the other name suggestions were the Dukes, the Cannons, the Stars, and the Wave.

"We were tied to the past, and the past wasn't necessarily something we wanted to be known for," Rays owner Stuart Sternberg said. "Nobody's running from it or hiding from it, and we're proud of certain aspects of it, but this is something the organization was able to really put their arms around. I hope and expect the fans who come out will see it as a new beginning."

That new beginning included T-shirts that were given to every player in spring training. On the shirts was an equation, 9=8. It was a slogan the team would adopt for the 2008 season. It meant: Play hard for nine innings and then the Rays will be one of eight playoff teams.

Not all were so optimistic going into the 2008 season. The Major League Baseball (MLB) playoffs usually take

Manager Joe Maddon guided the Rays from worst in 2007 to first in 2008 in the AL East Division.

place during October. But the facility managers at Tropicana Field were not expecting the Rays to still be playing in late October. So they booked Halloween Haunted Night events at the ballpark instead. They never anticipated that the Rays would have a breakout 2008 season.

The "new" Rays came from behind to win 45 games in 2008. Many of those comebacks were in the ninth inning. That helped the Rays cruise to a team-record 97 victories and a division title. For the first time in 11 years, a team other than the New York Yankees or Boston Red Sox won the AL East.

Carlos Pena gets mobbed by his teammates after scoring a game-winning run against the Baltimore Orioles during the 2008 season.

For the first time in Rays history, they were heading to the playoffs.

The Rays had gone from worst to first in one season. Young third baseman Evan Longoria was one of the main reasons. The 22-year-old drove in 85 runs and was named the AL Rookie of the Year. Pitcher James Shields had been a sixteenth-round draft choice. But he won a career-high 14 games with a 3.56 earned run average (ERA) in 2008. Fellow pitcher Scott Kazmir won 12 games.

Longoria was named to the All-Star Game that season. But besides him, the Rays did not have any dominant stars. No

Rays player ranked in the top nine in the AL in batting average, runs scored, runs batted in (RBIs), or home runs. None of the Rays' five starting pitchers eclipsed Shields' 14 wins. Yet somehow, Maddon transformed one of baseball's youngest and worst teams into one of its best. For that, he was named AL Manager of the Year.

"I knew we had something here," Kazmir said. "I knew we had the depth. I knew we had the pitching. I knew we had everything."

The Rays beat the Chicago White Sox three games to one in the AL Division Series (ALDS). The reigning World Series champion Red Sox awaited in the AL Championship Series (ALCS). Boston won the first game, but the Rays took the next three. Tampa Bay needed only one

TOP ROOKIE

When the Rays drafted Evan Longoria with the third pick of the 2006 draft, it took them just one day to sign him. Less than two years later, the third baseman made his big-league debut at age 22. He hit .272 during his rookie season. He also drove in 85 runs, hit 27 home runs, and made the All-Star team en route to being named the AL Rookie of the Year.

Longoria shined in the postseason. He hit home runs in his first two at-bats against the Chicago White Sox in the ALDS. That made him only the second player in major league history to hit homers in his first two postseason appearances. Then he hit four home runs in the ALCS against the Red Sox, including one each in three consecutive games at Boston's Fenway Park.

"Honestly, I wasn't surprised," Rays manager Joe Maddon said. "He likes these moments in a non-cocky way. He's just very confident."

more win to advance to the World Series. However, the Red Sox did not give up. They won the next two games, forcing the all-or-nothing seventh game.

The Red Sox had bullied the Rays since they came into the league in 1998. But this was Tampa Bay's year. Game 7 took place at Tropicana Field, and the Rays were ready.

Rays pitcher Matt Garza held the Red Sox to just two runs over seven innings. Rays designated hitter Willy Aybar scored the go-ahead run in the fifth inning. Then he added a solo home run in the seventh. The Rays won 3–1.

Rays second baseman Akinori Iwamura touched second base to force the last out in the ninth inning, securing the pennant for Tampa. He jumped high into the air. Within seconds, Rays players sprinted out onto the field and wound up in a celebratory pile on the ground behind the pitching mound. The players soon donned specially made blue AL championship T-shirts. Garza lifted his ALCS Most Valuable Player (MVP) trophy above his head for all to see.

The magical 2008 season ended in the World Series. The Rays fell to the powerful National League (NL) champion Philadelphia Phillies in five games. The Rays kept it close for the first three games,

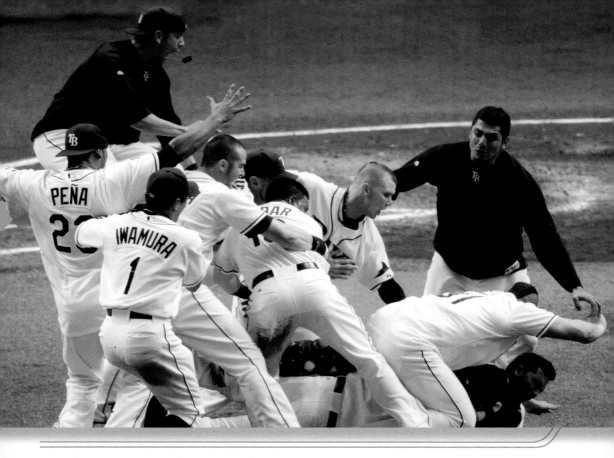

Rays players celebrate after defeating the Boston Red Sox 3–1 in Game 7 of the ALCS on October 19, 2008.

and they won Game 2 at Tropicana Field. But the Phillies pulled away with a 10–2 win in Game 4 and a tight 4–3 win in Game 5 to take the World Series title.

It was not the ending that fans in Tampa had been hoping for. But the Rays' success in 2008 had changed the way people looked at the team. They were no longer the doormats of the AL East. With a young core of players and Maddon at the helm, the Rays would be contending for the pennant for years to come.

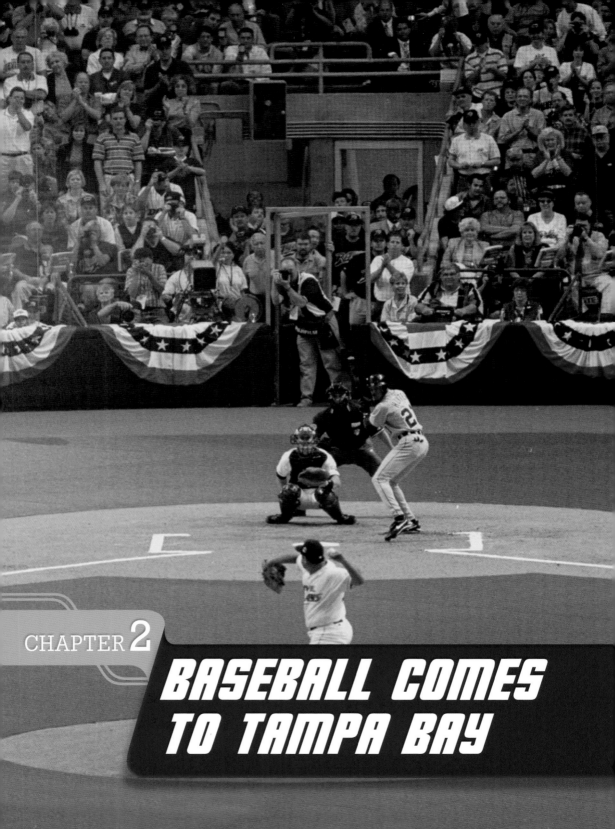

CHAPTER 2

BASEBALL COMES TO TAMPA BAY

Tampa and St. Petersburg are large cities that are separated by Tampa Bay on the sunny west coast of Florida. The cities were no strangers to baseball. Several major league teams held their spring training in the area. But by the time the temperatures heated up in the summer, the area was known more for its beaches than its baseball.

Al Lang Field was built in 1916 in St. Petersburg. It was the spring home to the St. Louis Cardinals since the 1940s and New York Mets since the 1960s. The Philadelphia Phillies trained in nearby Clearwater. The New York Yankees built Steinbrenner Field in Tampa in 1996. They had previously trained in St. Pete between 1925 and 1961. But Tampa and St. Pete baseball fans wanted their own major league team—one that would stay for the summer.

Tropicana Field in St. Petersburg officially welcomed baseball when Devil Rays pitcher Wilson Alvarez delivered the first pitch in team history on March 31, 1998.

FIRST MANAGER

The Devil Rays chose Larry Rothschild to be their first manager in 1998. He had been a star player for Florida State University's baseball team. Rothschild also got a brief taste of the major leagues. He pitched in just seven games over two seasons with the Detroit Tigers in 1981 and 1982, but never won a game.

However, Rothschild was a successful pitching coach in the majors. He was the Florida Marlins' pitching coach when they won the World Series in 1997. He also won a World Series ring as a coach for the Cincinnati Reds. Rothschild saw the Devil Rays job as a huge opportunity.

"These jobs don't come along very often," he said. "You don't get the opportunity to build from the ground up in very many situations." He was the Rays' manager for just more than three years, but did not have much success. The Rays went 205–294 during his time there.

The Florida Suncoast Dome opened in St. Petersburg in March 1990. It had cost $138 million to build. But it was a stadium without a team. The Suncoast Dome changed its name to the Thunderdome in 1993 with the arrival of the National Hockey League's Tampa Bay Lightning. Then the stadium became Tropicana Field in 1996 when the nearby Tropicana Dole Beverages Company sponsored it.

The Dome played host to many different events. Among them were Davis Cup tennis matches, college basketball games, karate competitions, sprint-car races, motorcycle races, track-and-field meets, and equestrian events. But the stadium was really built to host an MLB team.

In 1991, Vince Naimoli formed a group of Tampa Bay business people that sought

Vince Naimoli formed a group of business people that brought baseball to Tampa Bay in 1998.

to bring a team to Tropicana Field. The group tried to lure an existing team to Tampa Bay while also petitioning MLB to grant the city an expansion team. In 1991, baseball owners passed on Tampa Bay and decided to expand the NL into Miami and Denver. However, existing teams had previously expressed interest in moving there. That interest continued.

In 1988, it appeared that the Chicago White Sox were

Devil Rays third baseman Wade Boggs waits for a pitch during a 1998 game at Tropicana Field.

ready to move to the area. But that plan fizzled when the White Sox persuaded Chicago to help them build a new ballpark. The Seattle Mariners were briefly interested in moving to Tampa Bay in the early 1990s. But talks soon died off. The same thing happened with the Texas Rangers. Those talks broke down when the Rangers got a new ballpark in Arlington, Texas. It was a frustrating time for baseball fans in the area.

"Some teams were sincere about moving here," Naimoli

said. "Others used us for leverage."

Naimoli's group finally thought they had secured a team in 1992. They had negotiated a deal to purchase the San Francisco Giants for $115 million and move them to Florida. But the NL owners blocked the sale. They did not want to see San Francisco lose its team. Naimoli threatened a lawsuit, but he was told to be patient and wait for another round of MLB expansion.

Finally, on March 9, 1995—more than five years after the Suncoast Dome opened—Naimoli was awarded an AL expansion team. He would have to pay $130 million for the team. It would begin play in 1998.

Tropicana Field closed in 1996 and underwent an $85 million renovation. It took 17 months to complete. The stadium was made to be baseball ready. The team installed batting cages and pitching machines in the entertainment complex and created a baseball park that included shorter power alleys in left and right fields.

The big day arrived on March 31, 1998. More than 45,000 fans turned out to watch the Devil Rays play their first game against the Detroit Tigers. The Rays lost 11–6. But they won the next two games in the series.

Tampa Bay's first team had a mix of the old and new.

Historic Opening Day

Wilson Alvarez was the Rays' Opening Day starter when they debuted in the AL on March 31, 1998. However, the Detroit Tigers recorded most of the "firsts" at Tropicana Field that day. Tigers batter Tony Clark got the first hit and Luis Gonzalez hit the first home run. The Tigers also got the first win in Tropicana Field.

The lineup included third baseman Wade Boggs. He had been a star with the Boston Red Sox and New York Yankees. Boggs hit the Devil Rays' first home run in the opening game. Four-time All-Star first baseman Fred McGriff came over from the Atlanta Braves. He led the Devil Rays with a .284 batting average and 81 RBIs. Pitcher Rolando Arrojo, a 29-year-old rookie from Cuba, won 14 games. He was Tampa Bay's first All-Star.

The Devil Rays lost 99 games during their first year and finished a staggering 51 games behind the Yankees in the AL East. But Rays fans could find solace in this fun-filled fact: The Rays lost nine fewer games than the Florida Marlins, who had won the World Series the previous year.

Rolando Arrojo, a 29-year-old rookie from Cuba, won 14 games in 1998 and was the Devil Rays' first All-Star.

CHAPTER 3

DEVILISH
BEGINNINGS

The second season in Tampa was not much better than the first. The Devil Rays lost 93 games and again finished in the bottom of the AL East. A pennant was nowhere in sight for the young ball club.

While the Devil Rays struggled in the standings, the fans found other reasons to get excited about their team. The Rays had signed former AL MVP Jose Canseco before the season. The outfield slugger dazzled fans by hitting a team-high 34 home runs. Nineteen of them came during the first two months of the season. He also had 95 RBIs and was named to the AL All-Star team.

However, third baseman Wade Boggs was the Devil Rays' star attraction. Boggs had played 16 seasons with the Boston Red Sox and New York Yankees before signing with his hometown Rays in 1998. The future Hall of Famer was a career .328 hitter and a 12-time

Former AL MVP Jose Canseco signed with the Devil Rays prior to the 1999 season and led the team with 34 home runs that year.

All-Star. He was known for being one of the best hitters of his time.

Entering the 1999 season, Boggs needed 78 hits to reach 3,000 for his career. Devil Rays fans followed his chase for 3,000 throughout the season. Meanwhile, Boggs thought of his Tampa childhood. "All I could think of was Little League," Boggs said.

On August 7, 1999, the more than 39,000 fans at Tropicana Field got a treat. Boggs entered the game against the Cleveland Indians with 2,997 hits. After hitting two singles, Boggs was only one hit away from the benchmark number. Then, in the bottom of the sixth inning, Boggs slammed a home run to deep right field to get his 3,000th career hit.

Boggs pumped his fists after hitting the homer and pointed upward as he circled the bases, a tribute to his mother who died in a car accident in 1986. "How about that? First to reach 3,000 with a homer," Boggs said afterward.

Boggs retired after the 1999 season with 3,010 career hits. The team honored him by hosting a Wade Boggs Day at Tropicana Field. Even legendary Hall of Fame slugger Ted Williams showed up to honor Boggs.

The excitement surrounding Boggs in 1999 was replaced

No Kiss for 3,000

Wade Boggs became the first player in major league history to hit a home run for his 3,000th career hit. When he ran by Devil Rays' first base coach Billy Hatcher, he high-fived Hatcher, who may have been expecting more. "Billy had said that he wanted to kiss me on the 3000th, so I just ran by him so I didn't have to kiss him," Boggs said. Boggs did kiss home plate, and the Tropicana Field groundskeepers later dug the plate up and gave it to Boggs.

Wade Boggs hits a home run for his 3,000th career hit on August 7, 1999, at Tropicana Field.

by Fred McGriff's home-run swing in 2000. When McGriff hit a homer in Toronto in September 2000, he became the second player in baseball history to hit 200 home runs in both the AL and NL. However, the Rays barely improved from their dismal 1999 season. They had a 69–92 record. Things got even worse in 2001 and 2002, when the Rays lost 100 and 106 games, respectively.

Despite Boggs's chase of 3,000 hits and the home run swings of McGriff and Canseco, the Devil Rays' home attendance began to drop.

24

In the team's second year, overall attendance dropped by 1 million. By 2003, the Rays averaged just 13,070 fans per game. That ranked them last in the AL in attendance. Rays owner Vince Naimoli blamed the shrinking number of fans on the team's poor record and the fact that Tropicana Field is located approximately 20 miles (32.2 km) from downtown Tampa.

"We're not convenient to the bulk of our potential base," Naimoli told MLB Commissioner Bud Selig.

THE ROOKIE

Perhaps the most famous rookie in Rays history was Jimmy Morris. The high school baseball coach from Texas went to an open tryout during the 1999 season and caught the attention of Rays' scouts. Morris made his major league debut a few months later, on September 18, 1999, at age 35. He struck out the only batter he faced in a loss against the Rangers in Texas.

Morris appeared in 21 games for the Rays during the 1999 and 2000 seasons. He struck out 13 batters and had a 4.80 ERA. However, he never registered a win or a loss. Morris later wrote a book, *The Oldest Rookie*, which also inspired the 2002 movie, *The Rookie*. Actor Dennis Quaid played Morris in the film.

"God has a funny way of bringing some things around and knocking you in the head with the ultimate destination," Morris said.

In 2000, Fred McGriff used his powerful home-run swing to become the second player in history to hit 200 home runs in both the AL and the NL.

CHAPTER 4

RAYS ON THE RISE

The Devil Rays remained at the bottom of the standings during the early 2000s. However, the key pieces of a different Rays club were beginning to fall into place. It would simply take time to establish a winner.

Speedy left fielder Carl Crawford made his major league debut in 2002. That was the same year that the Rays selected outfielder B. J. Upton with their first pick in the draft. Crawford and Upton would soon make up one of the fastest outfield combinations in MLB.

In 2004, the Rays traded for Scott Kazmir. He was one of the New York Mets' top pitching prospects. In 2006, the Rays drafted third baseman Evan Longoria. All four of those players would play key roles as the Devil Rays developed into pennant contenders.

In 2003, however, the Rays were still in the cellar of the AL East. Through five seasons, the team had never finished better

Carl Crawford, *left*, and B. J. Upton provided the Rays with speed and power in the outfield. Crawford debuted with the Rays in 2002 while Upton debuted in 2004.

SWEET LOU COMES HOME

When Lou Piniella was hired as manager of the Devil Rays before the 2003 season, he was a perfect hometown choice. Piniella is a native of Tampa and attended high school at Tampa Jesuit. His college years were at the University of Tampa. Sweet Lou, as he was known, had won a World Series title with the Cincinnati Reds. Now he was coming home when he left the Seattle Mariners for the Rays.

"I believe in hard work, I believe in dedication. I believe in taking a tremendous amount of pride in the uniform that you wear in the city that you represent," he said upon joining the Rays.

Piniella led the Rays to a club-record 70 wins in 2004, but in 2005 the Rays lost 95 games and were in last place in the AL East again. Piniella questioned Tampa Bay's commitment to winning, and was released from his four-year contract one year early.

than its 69–92 record in 2000. So the Rays brought in fiery manager Lou Piniella. He had guided the Cincinnati Reds to a World Series title and had twice been the AL Manager of the Year.

Piniella's presence did little to help the Rays during his first season. The team won eight more games than it had in 2002. But the Rays still finished a dismal 63–99 and last in the AL East. It was the sixth consecutive year that the Rays had finished last.

Still, the Rays entered the 2004 season with optimism. "We're the most improved team in this division, period," Piniella said as spring training opened. They soon made a case for Piniella's claim.

The Rays began the 2004 season by beating the New York Yankees in a special game that took place in Tokyo,

Rocco Baldelli instructs children on a Japanese baseball team during the Devil Rays' 2004 visit to the US Naval Base in Yokosuka, southwest of Tokyo.

Japan. However, entering June, they were only 18–31. But then they got hot. The Rays won 20 of 26 games in June, including a club-record 12 straight. They were unable to keep that pace for the rest of the season. But they finished the season with a 70–91 record. It was their best record to date, and it was also the first time they finished above last in the AL East. They held off the Toronto Blue Jays by three games to finish fourth out of the five teams. However, the Rays were still 30 1/2 games

Devil Rays infielder Aubrey Huff connects for one of his team-high 29 home runs in 2004.

behind the AL East champion Yankees.

Third baseman Aubrey Huff, along with young out-fielders Crawford and Rocco Baldelli, paced the Devil Rays. Huff batted .297 with 29 home runs and 104 RBIs—leading the team in all three categories.

Crawford became a speed demon at Tropicana Field. He led the AL with 59 stolen bases and scored a team-high 104 runs. He was named to the

All-Star Game in 2004. Baldelli, meanwhile, batted .280 with 16 homers and 74 RBIs. Both Crawford and Baldelli were 22 years old in 2004, giving Rays fans hope for the future.

As promising as the 2004 season was, the Devil Rays soon sank back to the bottom of the AL East. They had a terrible start in 2005, winning just eight games on the road in the first half of the season. The Rays eventually lost 95 games. The team said farewell to the frustrated Piniella after that season. He criticized the team's new owner, Stuart Sternberg, for having the smallest payroll in the major leagues.

The team brought in new manager Joe Maddon for the 2006 season. Things got worse before they got better. While suffering through a rash of injuries, the Rays lost 101 games that season—the third

A New Owner

Stuart Sternberg grew up in Brooklyn, New York. He saw his first MLB game as a child with his dad in Shea Stadium. He assumed a majority ownership of the Devil Rays on October 6, 2005. The team's first owner, Vincent Naimoli, remained a chairman emeritus on the board of directors. Sternberg led an effort to market the Devil Rays to portions of Florida outside the Tampa-St. Petersburg area, and he made the team the first in the major leagues to offer free parking for those carpooling to a home game. He also founded the Rays Baseball Foundation, which benefits youth.

time in six years that they had lost more than 100 games—and again finished last in the AL East. However, those following the team closely could see the team's young star power was beginning to take effect.

CHAPTER 5

MAKING STRIDES

The Devil Rays were in a dire place in 2007. After nine seasons in the AL, the Rays had never finished better than 70–91 and fourth in the five-team AL East. Then they began the 2007 season by losing five of their first seven games.

In the first two months of the season, the Rays had losing streaks of six, five, and four games. They were already 14 1/2 games back in the AL East by the end of May.

The Rays finished the season with a 66–96 record, the worst in the majors. They were 30 games behind the AL East champion Boston Red Sox.

The Quickest Ray

Carl Crawford has virtually owned the base paths at Tropicana Field since his major league debut in 2002. He led the AL in stolen bases in four of his first six seasons, including 59 in 2004. Through 2010, he has led the AL in triples four times. And his speed has also helped him make big plays in left field. "Man, I just want to win," said Crawford, a four-time All-Star. "That's what I think about."

Scott Kazmir set a team record when he struck out 239 batters in 2007.

However, there were positive signs as the team looked again toward the future.

Starting pitchers Scott Kazmir and James Shields combined for 25 wins. Kazmir struck out a club-record 239 batters. Meanwhile, Shields became the third pitcher in franchise history to pitch 200 innings in one season. And Shields, at age 25, was the team's oldest starting pitcher.

New Bat in Town

When Carlos Pena arrived at the Devil Rays' spring-training camp in 2007, he was a man without a team. After a six-year major league career that had taken him to four different teams, Pena was a free agent in 2007. He quickly impressed Devil Rays manager Joe Maddon and the rest of the team management. Pena, a 29-year-old from the Dominican Republic, became the team's starting first baseman. He hit a career-high .282 in 2007 and played a major role in the Rays' 2008 AL pennant run.

The Rays had a potent young batting order, too. Both Carl Crawford and B. J. Upton hit better than .300. Crawford had 50 of the Rays' 131 stolen bases. That marked his fourth 50-steal season in five years. He was also the only Ray selected to the AL All-Star team.

The team had also added first baseman Carlos Pena before that season. He had played in just 18 games with the Red Sox in 2006. He won the starting job at first base and wound up hitting a club-record 46 home runs. He also drove in a career-high 121 runs. Pena was named the AL Comeback Player of the Year. Soon after, he was awarded a three-year, $24.125 million contract.

"It's awesome," Pena said of re-signing with the Rays. "It's extremely exciting. I get to be in a place I absolutely love, around people that I love and

B. J. Upton, *left*, greets Carlos Pena after one of Pena's 46 home runs in 2007. Pena had 121 RBIs that year.

people that I know care about me."

After getting off to a slow start in 2007, the Devil Rays showed some signs of life throughout the season. They finished 15–14 in August and went 11–16 in September. However, they did lose nine of their final 12 games.

Following the 2007 season, the Devil Rays changed their name to the Rays. They also changed their dominant color from green to blue. Few could have ever anticipated that the new-look Rays would cruise all the way to the World Series just one year later.

CHAPTER 6

THE NEW-LOOK RAYS

The celebration of the Rays' first AL pennant in 2008 brought new life to the franchise. Home crowds at Tropicana Field quickly increased. So did team and fan expectations. After such a dismal start to the team's existence, the 2008 name and color change truly did offer the Rays a fresh beginning.

The young Rays players who starred during the 2008 season continued to play well in 2009. With Joe Maddon managing the AL All-Stars, a record five Rays players made the team. That included the Rays' entire infield: first baseman Carlos Pena, second baseman Ben Zobrist, shortstop Jason Bartlett, and third baseman Evan Longoria. The fifth was left fielder Carl Crawford.

The Rays already had a young team, and more young stars emerged in 2009. Rookie pitchers David Price, Jeff Niemann, and Wade Davis

Evan Longoria's defensive play at third base helped him become one of five Rays All-Stars in 2009.

combined for 25 wins. Meanwhile, Pena tied for the AL lead in home runs with 39. Bartlett batted a team-high .320, placing him among the top 10 in the league. And Crawford stole a career-high 60 bases, finishing second in the AL. In a May game at home against the Boston Red Sox, Crawford tied a major league record by stealing six bases.

"He had a spectacular day," Red Sox manager Terry Francona said.

Those players led the Rays to a second consecutive winning season. But the New York Yankees were too much—for anybody. The Rays, at 84–78, finished 19 games behind the Yankees in the AL East. Even the rival Red Sox finished eight games back. So, for the Rays, it was worst-to-first-to-third, all within three years.

The defending AL champions never led the AL East in 2009. They began the season with a 5–3 loss in Boston, and wound up losing three of their first five games. A brutal 11-game losing streak in September ensured the Rays would not have a chance to defend their pennant in the playoffs.

Still, the Rays were optimistic going into the 2010 season.

"We've got everything," Crawford said. "We've definitely got all the pieces we need."

Rays pitcher Matt Garza received a motorcycle as a gift from his teammates after he threw the first no-hitter in franchise history on July 26, 2010.

The Rays began the 2010 season hot. They won their first two games against the Baltimore Orioles and then strung together a seven-game winning streak in April by sweeping the Orioles and Red Sox.

As the season cruised into the middle of June, Crawford's words proved accurate. The Rays and Yankees were tied for the best record in baseball at 40–23.

Many players stood out. Crawford and B. J. Upton combined for 41 steals in 63 games. In late July, Matt Garza pitched the first no-hitter in franchise history, a 5–0 win over the Detroit Tigers at Tropicana Field. Meanwhile, Price was establishing himself as one

The Rays rush the field after they beat the Baltimore Orioles 5–0 to clinch a 2010 playoff berth.

of the elite starting pitchers in the AL and Rafael Soriano was proving to be one of the elite closers. At season's end, Soriano had an AL-best 45 saves while Price finished 19–6 with a 2.72 ERA.

Those key performances also kept the Rays in the AL pennant chase all season. The Rays and the Yankees battled to the wire for the AL East title. The Rays finally won the division title with only two games to spare. They finished the season with a 96–66 record.

After 10 losing seasons as the Devil Rays, the new-look

Rays had three winning records in three seasons. Also, for the second time in three years, they were heading to the postseason.

"This team is number one," Pena said. "That's why we have this chemistry. We have a lot of heart."

Unfortunately for the Rays, that chemistry disappeared in the playoffs. The Rays hosted the AL West champion Texas Rangers for the first two games of the ALDS. But the Rangers won both of them. The Rays came back to win the next two games in Texas, but the Rangers won the deciding fifth game at Tampa Bay.

It was a disappointing loss for Rays fans. The team did not play with the grit and precision that it had during the regular season. But it was also disappointing because many of the Rays' star players were free agents at the end of the season.

Joe Maddon

Manager Joe Maddon helped turn the Rays from the AL East doormat to a force to be reckoned with in the AL. He also raised a few eyebrows along the way. His jersey number, 70, is the highest uniform number for a manager in major league history. And when he ordered an intentional walk of Texas Rangers slugger Josh Hamilton with the bases loaded in 2008, he was the first manager to do so in 107 years. "He has the personality of a teen-ager," former Rays pitcher Scott Kazmir said. "He fits in well with us."

The core of the group that had turned the Rays from one of the worst teams in the AL to one of the best teams was beginning to split apart.

However, the Rays still have some of the top young players in baseball. Behind Longoria and Price, the Rays are no longer overlooked as a contender in the powerful AL East.

TIMELINE

1990
The Florida Suncoast Dome opens on March 3. It would be more than eight years before the Devil Rays would make their debut in the stadium, then called Tropicana Field.

1995
Baseball owners vote to award the Tampa-St. Petersburg area an MLB franchise on March 9. The team would be called the Tampa Bay Devil Rays and play at Tropicana Field.

1998
The Devil Rays play the first regular-season game in franchise history in front of 45,369 at Tropicana Field, which had undergone an $85 million renovation, on March 31. However, the Rays lose to the Detroit Tigers, 11–6.

1998
Rolando Arrojo, a rookie pitcher, is the first Devil Rays All-Star. He pitches in one inning, giving up zero runs, in the AL's 13–8 win over the NL.

1999
Tampa native and Devil Rays third baseman Wade Boggs hits a home run for his 3,000th career hit, at Tropicana Field on August 7. It is his third hit of the night. As he crosses home plate, he kneels down and kisses it.

1999
Jimmy Morris, a Texas schoolteacher who was discovered in an open tryout camp, makes his big-league debut in a game at the Texas Rangers on September 18.

2002
The Devil Rays hire Tampa native Lou Piniella as the third manager in club history on October 28. Piniella led the Rays to what was then a club-record 70 wins in 2004, the second of his three seasons with the Rays.

2007
Devil Rays pitcher Scott Kazmir strikes out a club-record 13 batters in a 14–3 win over the Oakland Athletics on August 25.

2007	The Devil Rays change their name to the Rays and change their team colors from green to blue in a downtown rally on November 8.
2008	Third baseman Evan Longoria hits two home runs, leading the Rays to their first postseason win, 6–4 over the Chicago White Sox, on October 2.
2008	The Rays defeat the Boston Red Sox 3–1 in Game 7 of the ALCS on October 19, giving Tampa Bay its first AL pennant.
2008	The first World Series game is played at Tropicana Field on October 22. The Rays lose to the Philadelphia Phillies, 3–2.
2008	B. J. Upton steals three bases in Game 3 of the World Series on October 25, tying a Series single-game record. The Rays' 22 stolen bases in the postseason break the major league record.
2009	Rays outfielder Carl Crawford steals six bases in a game against the Red Sox on May 3 at Tropicana Field, tying a major league record.
2010	Rays pitcher Matt Garza throws the first no-hitter in team history on July 26 at Tropicana Field. Only a walk in the second inning prevents him from throwing a perfect game against the Tigers.
2010	The Rays hold off the New York Yankees to win the AL East Division title. However, in the playoffs the Rays lose the first two games to the Rangers and eventually lose the series 3–2.

QUICK STATS

FRANCHISE HISTORY

Tampa Bay Devil Rays (1998–2007)
Tampa Bay Rays (2008–)

WORLD SERIES
(wins in bold)

2008

AL CHAMPIONSHIP SERIES
(1969–)

2008

DIVISION CHAMPIONSHIPS
(1969–)

2008, 2010

WILD-CARD BERTHS

None

KEY PLAYERS
(position; seasons with team)

Rolando Arrojo (SP; 1998–99)
Rocco Baldelli (OF; 2003–04,
    2006–08, 2010)
Jason Bartlett (SS; 2008–)
Wade Boggs (3B; 1998–99)
Jose Canseco (OF; 1999–2000)
Carl Crawford (OF; 2002–)
Matt Garza (SP; 2008–)
Scott Kazmir (SP; 2004–09)
Evan Longoria (3B; 2008–)
Fred McGriff (1B; 1998–2001, 2004)
Carlos Pena (1B; 2007–)
David Price (SP; 2008–)
James Shields (SP; 2006–)
B. J. Upton (OF; 2004–)

KEY MANAGERS

Joe Maddon (2006–)
    404–406; 10–11 (postseason)
Lou Piniella (2003–05):
    200–285
Larry Rothschild (1998–2001):
    205–294

HOME FIELDS

Tropicana Field (1998–)

* Statistics through 2010 season

QUOTES AND ANECDOTES

There are plenty of stories of players losing sight of fly balls against the bright ceiling of Tropicana Field, a stadium described as "a giant inflated white pillow" by Devil Rays pitcher Jimmy Morris in his book, *The Oldest Rookie*. But what about the ball that never came down? It happened on May 2, 1999, when Rays slugger Jose Canseco whacked a ball high into the air. When it came down, the ball hit a catwalk and stayed there. Canseco was awarded a double.

When Hall of Famer Wade Boggs arrived in Tampa Bay in 1998, he brought all his superstitions with him. He ate fried chicken before every game. He took batting practice before every night game at 5:17 p.m. He woke up at the same time every day. Upon his retirement, he told a reporter: "To be honest, it was sort of a relief when I retired and I didn't have to keep up all of those rituals."

"You don't get 3,000 hits in this game, buddy, without being one [heck] of a hitter."—Ted Williams, at age 80, speaking at Wade Boggs Day on August 23, 1999, at Tropicana Field. Boggs finished his career with 3,010 hits.

Kevin Costner, an actor whose baseball roles included Crash Davis in *Bull Durham* and Ray Kinsella in *Field of Dreams*, became a part of Rays baseball lore when he and his band, Modern West, created a song, "It's All Up to You," during the 2008 championship season. He was a big fan of Rays manager Joe Maddon. "[He] didn't make it into the bigs as a player and . . . I kind of dig that," Costner said. "That's kind of who Crash Davis was."

"We can still feel Lou around here. I know I can."—Rays outfielder Carl Crawford, talking about former Rays manager Lou Piniella

GLOSSARY

contract

A binding agreement about, for example, years of commitment by a baseball player in exchange for a given salary.

designated hitter

A position used only in the American League. Managers can employ a hitter in the batting order who comes to the plate to hit instead of the pitcher.

draft

A system used by professional sports leagues to select new players in order to spread incoming talent among all teams.

expansion

In sports, the addition of a franchise or franchises to a league.

franchise

An entire sports organization, including the players, coaches, and staff.

free agent

A player whose contract has expired and who is able to sign with a team of his choice.

legendary

Well known and admired over a long period.

payroll

The total amount paid to all the players on the team.

pennant

A flag. In baseball, it symbolizes that a team has won its league championship.

postseason

The games in which the best teams play after the regular-season schedule has been completed.

prospect

A young player, usually one who has little major league experience.

FOR MORE INFORMATION

Further Reading

Isaacson, Melissa. *Sweet Lou: Lou Piniella, a Life in Baseball*. Chicago: Triumph Books, 2009.

Morris, Jim, and Joel Engel. *The Oldest Rookie*. Boston: Little Brown & Co., 2001.

Vecsey, George. *Baseball: A History of America's Favorite Game*. New York: Modern Library, 2008.

Web Links

To learn more about the Tampa Bay Rays, visit ABDO Publishing Company online at **www.abdopublishing.com**. Web sites about the Rays are featured on our Book Links page. These links are routinely monitored and updated to provide the most current information available.

Places to Visit

Charlotte Sports Park
2300 El Jobean Rd.
Port Charlotte, FL 33948
941-235-5010
www.charlottecountyfl.com/
CommunityServices/ParkPages/
SportsPark/
This has been the Rays' spring-training ballpark since 2009.

National Baseball Hall of Fame and Museum
25 Main Street
Cooperstown, NY 13326
888-HALL-OF-FAME
www.baseballhall.org
This hall of fame and museum highlights the greatest players and moments in the history of baseball. Wade Boggs is the only former Rays player enshrined there.

Tropicana Field
One Tropicana Drive
St. Petersburg, FL 33705
888-326-7297
tampabay.rays.mlb.com/tb/ballpark/
index.jsp
This has been the Rays' home field since 1998. The stadium features the Rays Tank, an aquarium located behind center field.

INDEX

About the Author

Paul Bowker is a freelance writer and author based in Ponte Vedra, Florida, and a frequent visitor to Tampa. His 25-year newspaper career includes several years as deputy sports editor at the *Florida Times-Union*. He has covered four World Series. He has won many national, regional, and state awards as a writer and editor, and he is a past president of Associated Press Sports Editors. He lives with his wife and daughter.